W9-COY-741

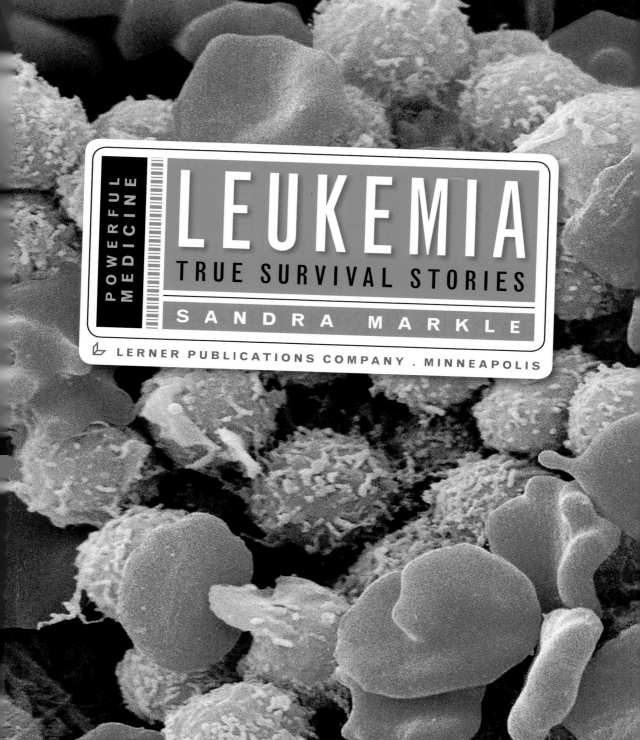

POWERFUL MEDICINE

LEUKEMIA
TRUE SURVIVAL STORIES

SANDRA MARKLE

LERNER PUBLICATIONS COMPANY . MINNEAPOLIS

NOTE FROM THE AUTHOR

The books in the Powerful Medicine series are the result of exciting detective work that let me talk to amazing, caring physicians, surgeons, and researchers. I also got to know patients who faced challenging, life-changing experiences with determination and courage. I consider all the people you'll meet in the Powerful Medicine series heroes and their stories remarkable. Those you'll meet in *Leukemia* are also courageous. They are children who continued to smile and find joy in living even when treatment, for a time, made them feel worse rather than better. From them, I've learned the true meaning of hope.

FOR CURIOUS KIDS EVERYWHERE—THEY'RE THE FUTURE!

Acknowledgments: The author would like to thank the following people for taking the time to share their expertise: Dr. Terzah Horton, Pediatric Hematology-Oncology, Baylor College of Medicine; Dr. Michael Lill, Hematology-Oncology, Cedars-Sinai Medical Center; Dr. Judith Marcus, Pediatric Hematology-Oncology, Columbia Presbyterian Hospital; Dr. Sonja Nodland, Masonic Cancer Center, University of Minnesota; Dr. Michael Sullivan, Children's Cancer Research Group, Christchurch Hospital, New Zealand; and Dr. Zoann Dreyer, Pediatric Hematology-Oncology, Texas Children's Cancer Center And Hematology Service Clinic. A special thank you to Skip Jeffery for his loving support during the creative process.

The cover image shows healthy lymphocytes (white blood cells). The title page image shows leukemic lymphocytes.

Lerner Publications Company
A division of Lerner Publishing Group, Inc.
241 First Avenue North
Minneapolis, MN 55401 U.S.A.

Website address: www.lernerbooks.com

Library of Congress Cataloging-in-Publication Data

Markle, Sandra.
    Leukemia: true survival stories / by Sandra Markle.
    p. cm. — (Powerful medicine)
    Includes bibliographical references and index.
    ISBN 978–0–8225–8700–2 (lib. bdg. : alk. paper)
    1. Leukemia—Juvenile literature. I. Title.
RC643.M346 2011
616.99'419—dc22   2009034441

Manufactured in the United States of America
1 - DP - 7/15/10

CONTENTS

We never think much about how our bodies work to keep us healthy and active. Then when something happens to one body part, we realize how important it is. **This book is about one of those key parts— the blood.** It is also about what happens to people when they get a blood disease called leukemia. Leukemia is the name for different kinds of cancers that affect the body's blood cells. In this book, you will read real-life stories of people with leukemia. The stories tell how doctors and researchers helped save the lives of people with leukemia, and how science and technology help in the fight.

WHAT'S WRONG WITH PAUL?

IN 2004, WHEN PAUL LUISI WAS ELEVEN, HIS WHOLE LIFE REVOLVED AROUND PLAYING SPORTS. When Paul began to feel tired, his parents thought it was just because he was playing too hard. **But then he started complaining of a stiff neck and feeling ill, so his mother, Diane, took him to the doctor.** This general checkup showed only that Paul had flulike symptoms. The doctor suggested Paul take time off from sports to rest until he felt better. But Paul didn't improve. So his mother took him back to the doctor. **This time the doctor ordered a blood test. He was checking for signs of an infection.**

Normally, a blood sample has many more red blood cells *(brown)* than white blood cells *(stained blue)*. But, like the sample on the bottom, Paul's blood sample had lots of white blood cells—many more than normal. There were even more than could be expected if Paul had an infection. Diane Luisi said, "Not in my wildest dreams did I suspect the diagnosis we were given. We were told Paul probably had leukemia."

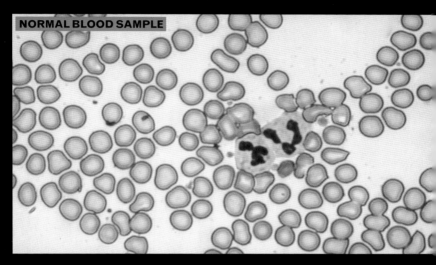

NORMAL BLOOD SAMPLE

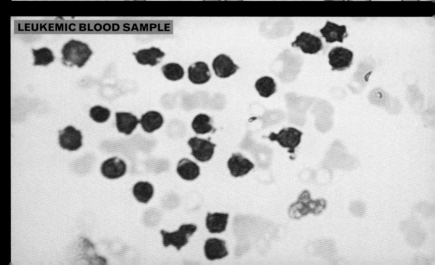

LEUKEMIC BLOOD SAMPLE

WHAT IS LEUKEMIA?

LEUKEMIA IS A KIND OF CANCER. CANCER IS A GROUP OF DISEASES CAUSED BY THE BODY'S OWN CELLS MULTIPLYING OUT OF CONTROL. Sometimes cancer causes tumors, or lumplike growths. Other times cancer causes some body part to stop working the way it usually does. **In leukemia, some blood cells multiply too quickly. This happens because of problems in the red bone marrow.**

Bones are hard, but they aren't solid. Many bones have a central cavity, or hole, filled with a soft, spongy tissue called bone marrow. There are two kinds of bone marrow, yellow and red. Yellow bone marrow is mainly fat. Red bone marrow contains special blood-forming stem cells. These stem cells make new blood cells. In children, most bones contain red bone marrow. In adults, about half of all bone marrow is yellow. Red bone marrow in adults is found mainly in flat bones.

CHILD'S LONG BONE CONTAINING RED MARROW

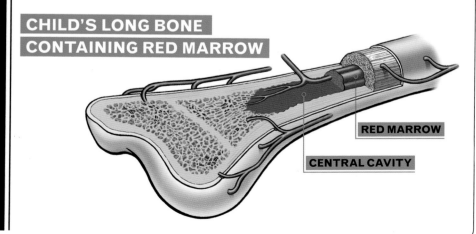

RED MARROW

CENTRAL CAVITY

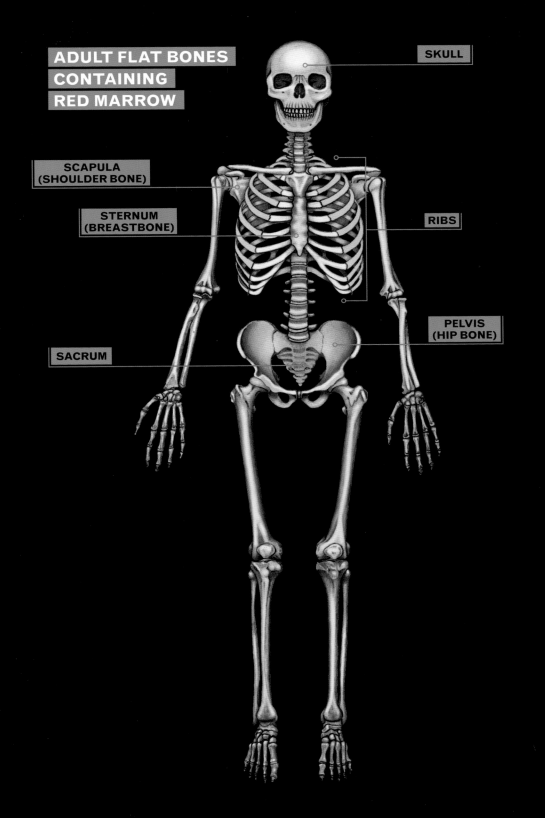

ADULT FLAT BONES CONTAINING RED MARROW

SKULL

SCAPULA (SHOULDER BONE)

STERNUM (BREASTBONE)

RIBS

SACRUM

PELVIS (HIP BONE)

Like all body cells, blood cells wear out and die. New blood cells are being made all the time. Usually, the body has just the right number of three kinds of blood cells: red blood cells, white blood cells, and platelets. Each of these has its own job to do for a person to be healthy. But for some reason no one understands, sometimes the blood-forming cells, called stem cells, stop working normally. Then they make too few red blood cells and platelets and too many white blood cells. Worse, many of the white blood cells aren't normal, healthy cells. When this happens to someone, they have leukemia. Each year about 250,000 people worldwide get leukemia.

Photo by Dr. Richard Kassel & Dr. Randy Kardon/
Tissues & Organs/Visuals Unlimited, Inc.

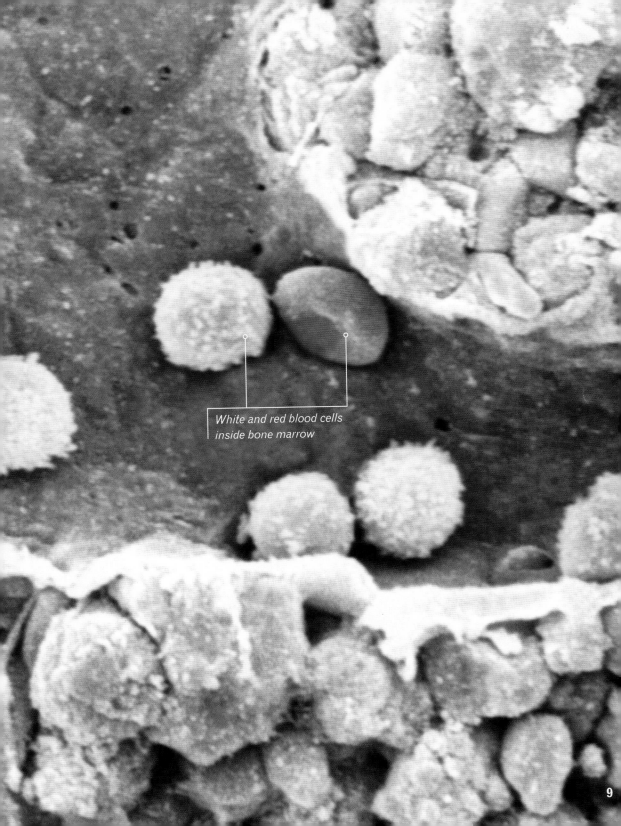

White and red blood cells
inside bone marrow

BLOOD MAKES UP ABOUT 7 PERCENT OF A PERSON'S BODY WEIGHT. An average adult has about 5 quarts (4.7 liters) of blood. Blood travels around the body through a network of blood vessels. It is pumped from the heart through arteries into tiny capillaries. Then the blood returns to the heart in the veins. Each of the three kinds of blood cells has a special job to do. Most of the cells are red blood cells, also called erythrocytes. They deliver oxygen to all the body's cells. They are red because they contain an iron-rich protein called hemoglobin. The iron in the cells combines with oxygen in the lungs. Then the oxygen is carried to anywhere the body needs it, such as the muscles.

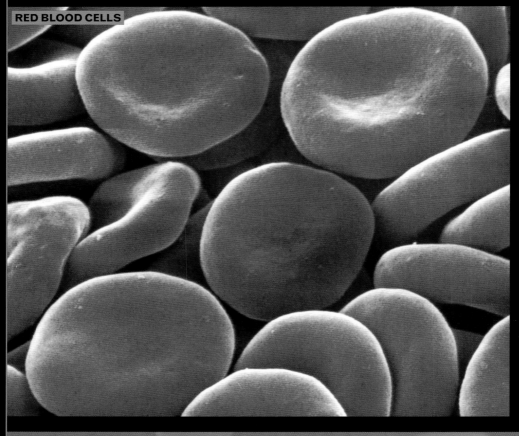

RED BLOOD CELLS

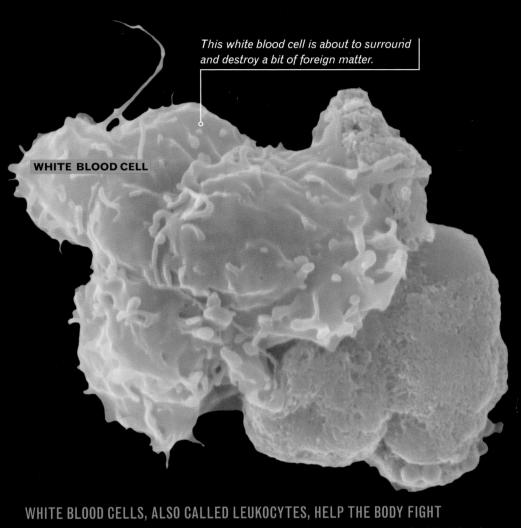

This white blood cell is about to surround and destroy a bit of foreign matter.

WHITE BLOOD CELL

WHITE BLOOD CELLS, ALSO CALLED LEUKOCYTES, HELP THE BODY FIGHT INFECTIONS AND DISEASES. There are a number of different kinds of white blood cells. Each attacks specific kinds of invaders, such as bacteria or viruses. White blood cells can leave the blood and squeeze through the blood vessel walls. Then they travel throughout the body, seeking out and attacking invaders.

PLATELETS, ALSO CALLED THROMBOCYTES, keep blood from leaking out of damaged blood vessels. Wherever blood is escaping—such as from a cut or a scrape—platelets release chemicals that attract more platelets. They produce netlike fibers that seal the opening and stop the leak.

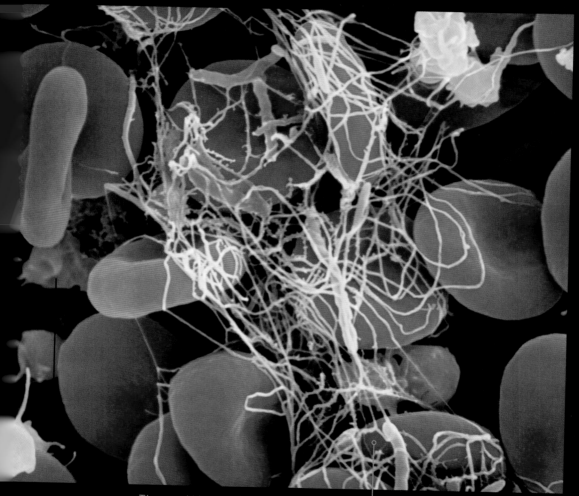

These red blood cells and platelets (colored blue) *form a scab. That seals the wound.*

To be sure Paul's problem was leukemia, his parents took him to the hospital for a bone marrow biopsy (study). First, Paul's skin was numbed over the test site on his back, just below the waist. A long, hollow, needlelike syringe was used to bore through his hip bone into the marrow. Like punching a straw into Jell-O, the syringe filled up with fluid and a little bit of the bone. Technicians examined a slide of this material under a microscope. They saw lots more white blood cells than normal. Many of these cells looked irregular. Paul definitely had leukemia.

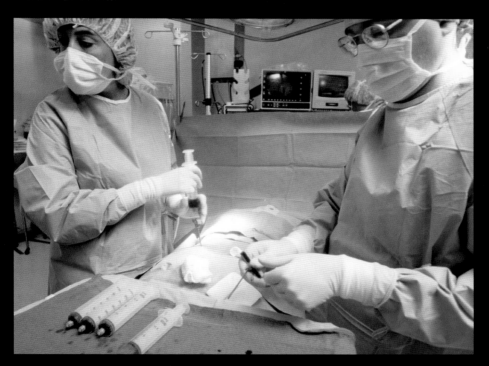

WHAT'S WRONG WITH BIANCA?

EARLY IN JUNE 2007, BIANCA WHITE CAME DOWN WITH A CASE OF TONSILLITIS, AN INFECTION OF HER TONSILS. Her family doctor gave her a drug to fight the infection, but Bianca didn't get better. In fact, she got worse. Then one afternoon, when Bianca's mother, Lea, was combing Bianca's hair, she felt a lump on her daughter's neck. She took Bianca back to the doctor for a checkup. He ordered a blood test. **The test showed that Bianca had too many white blood cells.** There were more than there should have been even to fight Bianca's tonsillitis. The doctor suspected she had leukemia. **Like Paul, she went to the hospital for a bone marrow biopsy.**

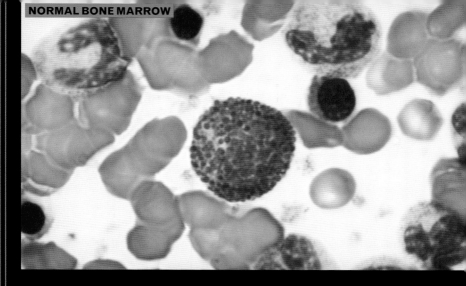

A sample of Bianca's bone marrow was collected from the back of her hip bone. Like the leukemic bone marrow sample below, Bianca's sample showed lots of abnormal white cells. She had leukemia too.

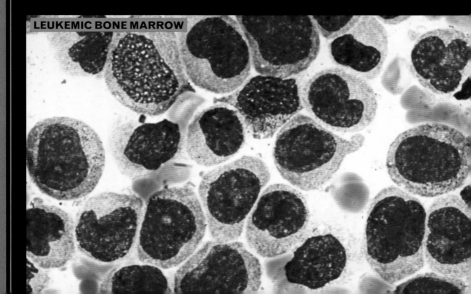

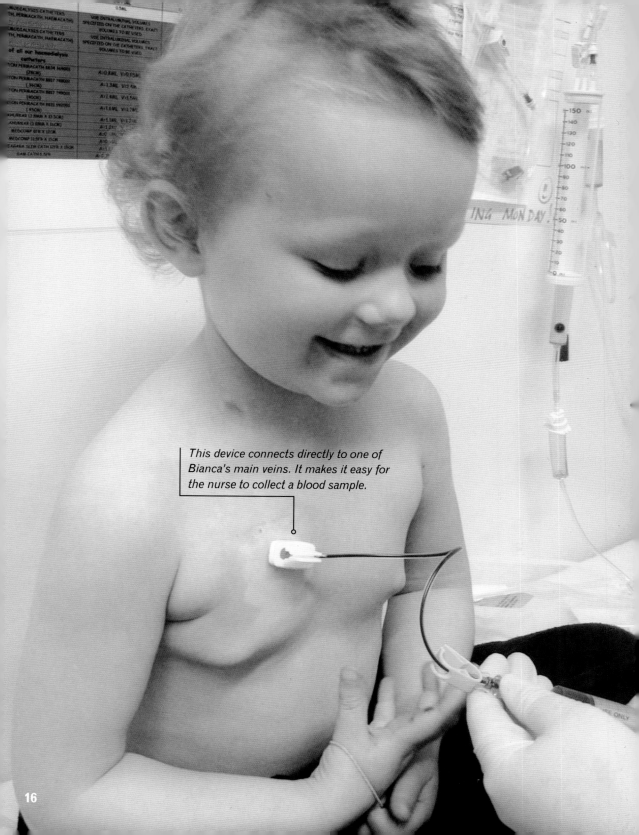

This device connects directly to one of Bianca's main veins. It makes it easy for the nurse to collect a blood sample.

CHEMOTHERAPY

DOCTORS OFTEN INSTALL A SPECIAL DEVICE THROUGH THE CHEST WALL OF A LEUKEMIA PATIENT. THE DEVICE CONNECTS TO ONE OF THE MAIN VEINS LEADING INTO THE HEART. Bianca quickly had surgery to install one of these devices. It helped Bianca's medical team collect blood samples more easily. They need the samples to keep track of the number of red blood cells, white blood cells, and platelets in her blood. The device was also a way for Bianca to receive big doses of special drugs. **This drug treatment for many kinds of cancer, including leukemia, is called chemotherapy.**

Dr. Michael Sullivan, part of Bianca's medical team said, "Chemotherapy remains a good treatment for leukemia because it works against a whole range of fast-growing cells in the body. There's no magic bullet treatment against leukemia because cancer cells change very rapidly. Even if one drug killed 99 percent of the leukemia cells, there would still be that 1 percent that's already changed. And those cells would continue to multiply."

When Paul was diagnosed with leukemia, he had a similar device installed in his chest. Then he too started chemotherapy. But the drugs Paul received were different from those given to Bianca. That's because Paul and Bianca had different kinds of leukemia. Red bone marrow has two kinds of blood-forming stem cells: myeloid and lymphoid. The type of leukemia someone develops depends on which of these two kinds of cells is affected. Paul's myeloid stem cells were involved, so he had myelogenous leukemia. Bianca's lymphoid stem cells caused the problem, so she had lymphocytic leukemia. Because their symptoms developed quickly, both had acute cases of their disease. If a leukemia patient's symptoms develop slowly, the disease is said to be chronic.

Like Bianca, nearly three-fourths of all children who develop leukemia have acute lymphocytic leukemia (ALL). Adults who develop leukemia most often have acute myelogenous leukemia (AML). In addition, some children, like Paul, get AML.

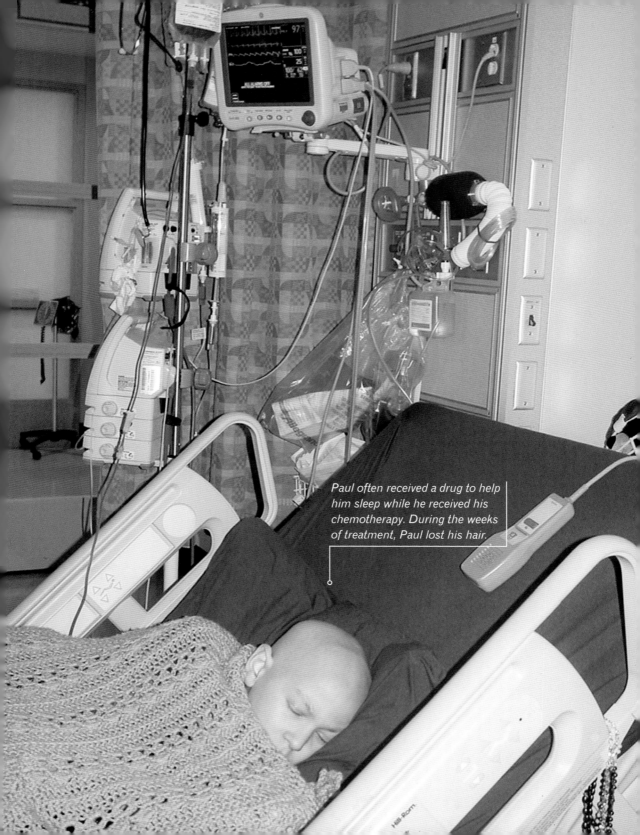

Paul often received a drug to help him sleep while he received his chemotherapy. During the weeks of treatment, Paul lost his hair.

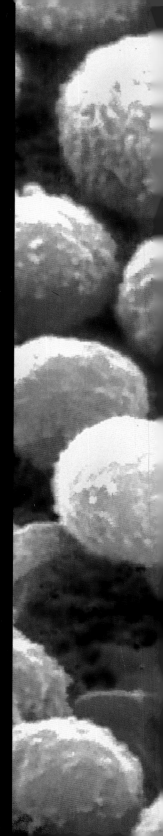

Although Paul and Bianca were treated with different drugs, all the chemotherapy drugs they received were very strong and given in big doses. Their treatments were meant to quickly wipe out the leukemic cells. The reason for this is that leukemic cells do something unusual. Normally, only stem cells in the bone marrow divide to produce new blood cells. But leukemic white blood cells also divide, creating more leukemic white blood cells.

Dr. Michael Sullivan said, "This happens over and over so quickly the bone marrow fills up with leukemic cells. The leukemic cells compete with the healthy cells for food nutrients and oxygen. Then many healthy blood-forming stem cells die."

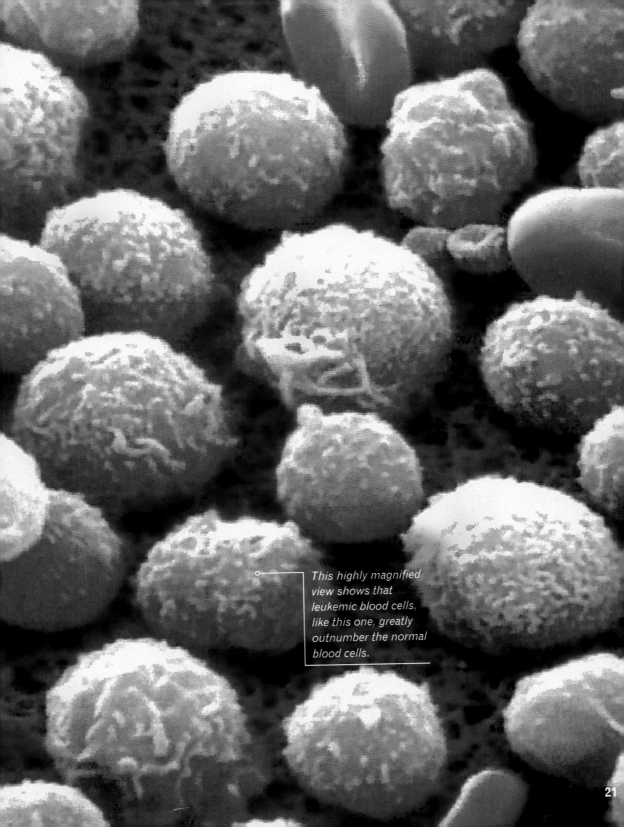

This highly magnified view shows that leukemic blood cells, like this one, greatly outnumber the normal blood cells.

Chemotherapy drugs work best on fast-growing cells. That's why these drugs kill the leukemic white blood cells. But skin cells, hair follicle cells, and the cells lining the stomach and intestines are fast-growing too. These cells are also affected by the chemotherapy drugs. That's why chemotherapy sometimes causes unpleasant side effects.

Paul said, "During chemotherapy, I remember often feeling like I had the flu: nauseous, achy, headachy. I also had mouth sores and didn't feel like eating a lot of the time. I couldn't stand to eat anything hard. My family was great, though, bringing me just about anything I asked for to eat."

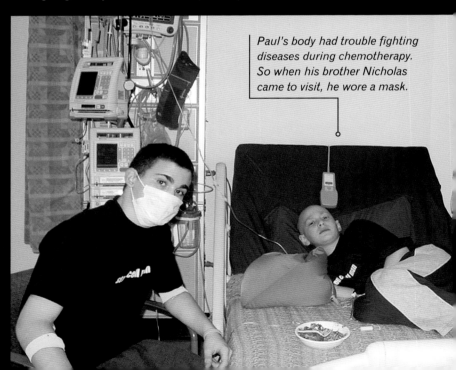

Paul's body had trouble fighting diseases during chemotherapy. So when his brother Nicholas came to visit, he wore a mask.

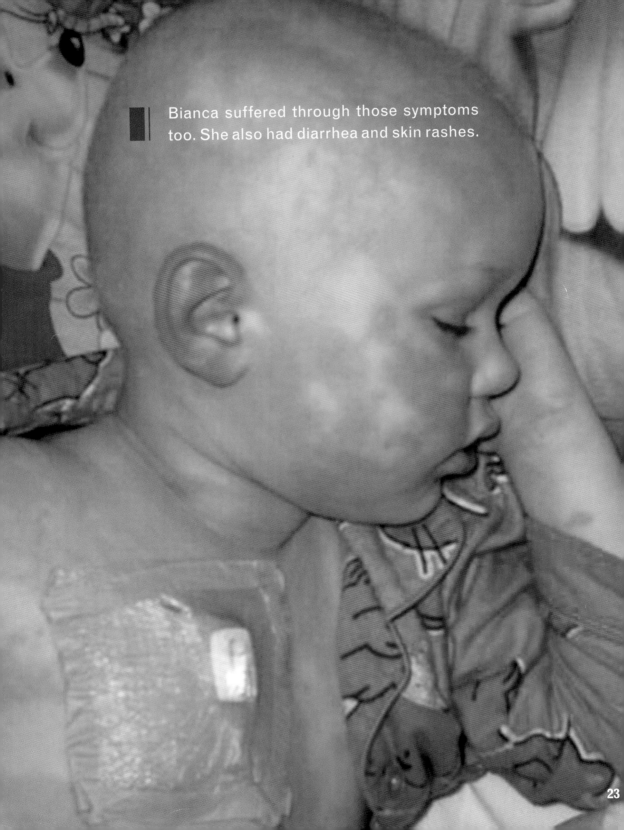

Bianca suffered through those symptoms too. She also had diarrhea and skin rashes.

The goal of chemotherapy is to stop the production of leukemic white blood cells. But the drugs also affect all blood cells. That can cause the patient to have too few red blood cells and platelets. So during their chemotherapy treatments, both Paul and Bianca needed transfusions (injections) of red blood cells and platelets. They could receive platelets from anyone. But red blood cells are not all the same. They had to come from someone with similar blood.

Paul's mother, Diane Luisi, said, "We so appreciated all of our friends lining up to donate blood in the direct donor program [blood donated especially for someone's use]. We never knew whose blood cells Paul received, but we were grateful for all of the support."

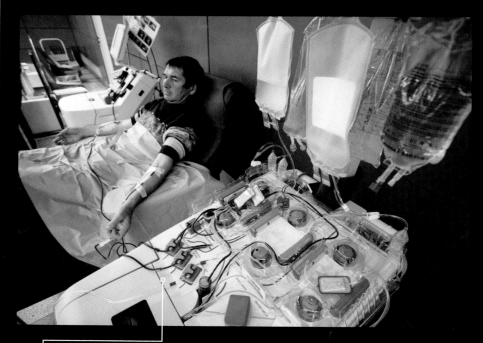

This person is donating his platelets. The blood is withdrawn from one arm, and the platelets are filtered out by the machine. Then the blood—minus the platelets—is returned through the other arm.

HUMAN BLOOD ISN'T ALL ALIKE.
Some people have blood that
contains certain proteins and other
substances, called antigens. Other
people's blood lacks these. Human
blood is divided into types, or groups,
called A, B, AB, and O. The presence
or absence of still other antigens
mean each of these types is divided
into two more groups. Those that
have antigens are positive. Those that
don't have antigens are negative. So,
for example, someone with Type A
blood will have either A+ or A− blood.
Receiving the wrong type blood in a
transfusion can be fatal. That is why
technicians carefully label donated
blood. Doctors and nurses check the
labels before the blood is used.

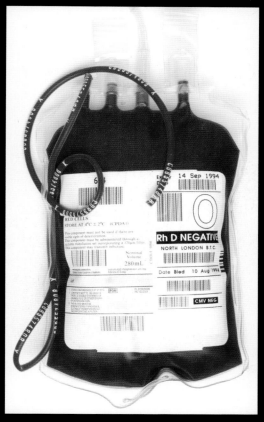

Chemotherapy also weakens the body's ability to fight diseases. That's because the drug kills nearly all the normal white blood cells along with the leukemic ones. So leukemia patients have to be protected from germs after receiving chemotherapy. Dr. Judith Marcus, Paul's doctor, said, "It can take about a month [after a chemotherapy treatment] for the bone marrow to turn on and begin producing enough white blood cells. To speed things up, we can give an injection that stimulates normal white blood cells to produce much faster."

Paul stayed in the hospital waiting for his white blood cell count to go up. His family and friends had to put on masks before visiting him. When Bianca's white blood cell count improved enough, she got to go home between rounds of chemotherapy treatment. Just to be on the safe side, though, she wore a mask (right) to protect her from breathing in any germs.

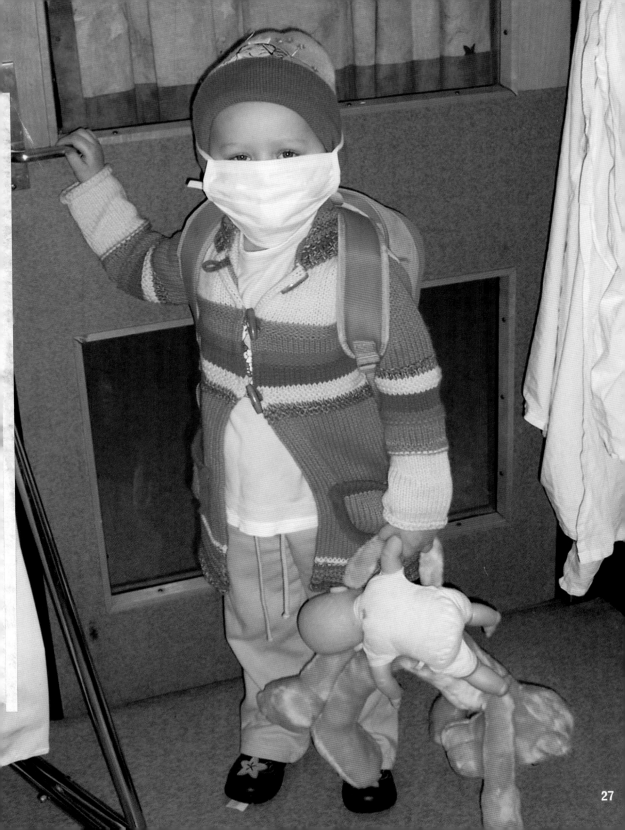

Like most leukemia patients, Paul and Bianca shared another common side effect of chemotherapy. They both lost their hair.

Paul's mother, Diane, said, "When Paul started to lose his hair, he got the rest shaved off. Later, to support him, so did Greg [his dad]. I must say I thought Paul looked quite handsome bald. Greg was another story."

HAIR HAS ITS FAST-GROWING CELLS IN THE HAIR FOLLICLE AT THE ROOT. Hairs get longer as stem cells at the root add on more living cells. Those cells die once they emerge from the surrounding skin layers. The hairs you see on your head and other body parts are made up of dead cells. Hair loss is a good sign that chemotherapy is doing its job. It's killing fast-growing cells, such as hair stem cells and cancer cells. But hair stem cells are especially hardy cells. Usually, at least some survive the chemotherapy treatment. So once chemotherapy is stopped, the surviving cells start producing more hair cells. Then the hair begins to grow again.

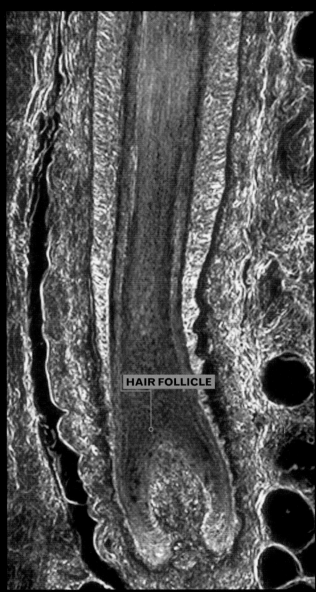

HAIR FOLLICLE

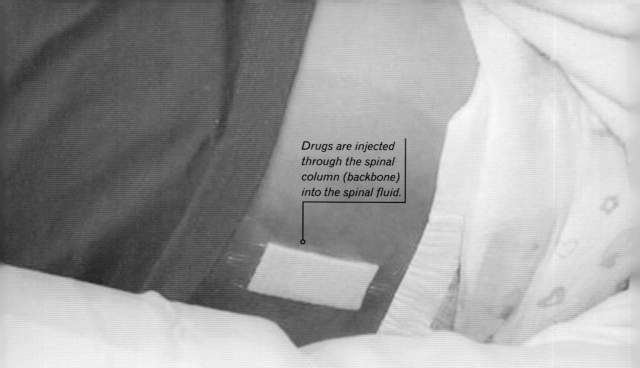

Drugs are injected through the spinal column (backbone) into the spinal fluid.

During treatment, both Paul and Bianca also received injections of chemotherapy drugs directly into their spinal fluid. This fluid is in a person's spinal column (backbone) and brain. The goal of this treatment is to kill any leukemic cells in the spinal fluid before they reach the brain. Chemotherapy drugs can't kill leukemic cells that reach the brain. The brain's leukemic cells are protected by a blood-brain barrier. Blood cells and food nutrients can pass through to reach the brain tissue's cells. But molecules of the chemotherapy drugs are too big to get through. The barrier blocks them. Any leukemic cells that reach the brain are protected from the chemotheraphy treatment.

Then, after the drug treatment stops, leukemic cells in the brain, which were protected by the blood-brain barrier, may travel throughout the body. They continue to divide to produce more leukemic cells. The leukemia would start all over again. The patient would suffer a relapse.

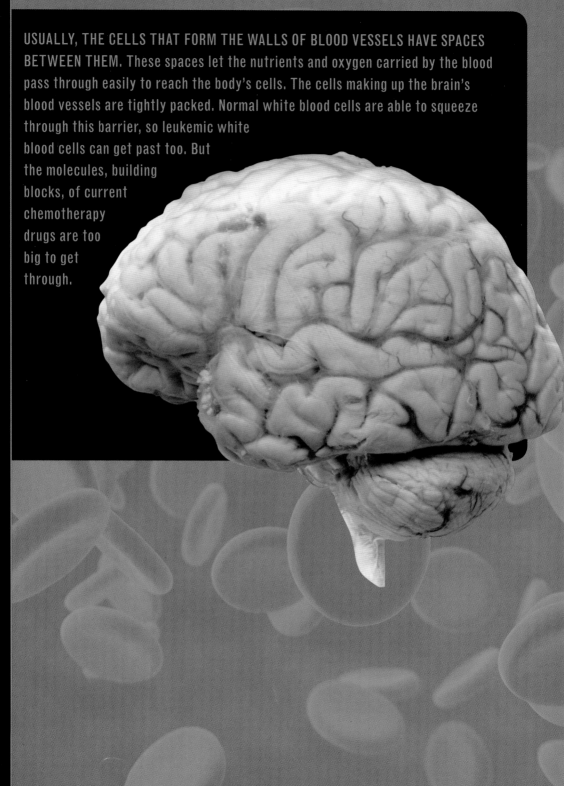

USUALLY, THE CELLS THAT FORM THE WALLS OF BLOOD VESSELS HAVE SPACES BETWEEN THEM. These spaces let the nutrients and oxygen carried by the blood pass through easily to reach the body's cells. The cells making up the brain's blood vessels are tightly packed. Normal white blood cells are able to squeeze through this barrier, so leukemic white blood cells can get past too. But the molecules, building blocks, of current chemotherapy drugs are too big to get through.

Bianca (left) wears a pretty bandana to cover her bald head. To show their support for her, her mother, Lea White, and sister, Caitlyn, also wear bandanas.

The first phase of chemotherapy is called the induction phase. It lasts until the patient goes into remission. Remission occurs when the number of leukemic cells in a bone marrow sample is less than 5 percent of the total cells counted. Next comes the consolidation phase. The goal of this phase is to keep the patient in remission. For AML patients, like Paul, these two stages are usually short—two weeks or less. For ALL patients, like Bianca, these first two phases of chemotherapy last about a month. Bianca's doctors felt that chemotherapy was all the treatment she needed. After completing the first two phases, she went home to continue the third phase, the maintenance phase. In this phase, she receives lower doses of drugs and is tested less often. Its goal is to keep her in remission for a long period—even the rest of her life. The maintenance phase lasts about two years.

STEM CELL TRANSPLANT

DR. MARCUS DIDN'T BELIEVE CHEMOTHERAPY WAS ENOUGH TO ENSURE PAUL'S KIND OF LEUKEMIA WOULD REMAIN IN REMISSION. He needed a blood-forming stem cell transplant. This involves putting someone else's healthy cells into his body. But everyone's blood-forming stem cells are different. Luckily, tests showed that Paul's older brother Nicholas had cells that were similar enough for a transplant.

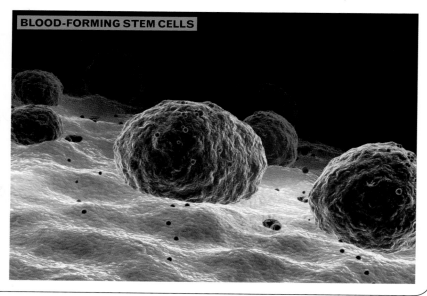

BLOOD-FORMING STEM CELLS

First, Nicholas took a special drug for five days. This made his bone marrow produce lots more blood-forming stem cells than usual. The extra stem cells passed into his bloodstream. Then Nicholas (below) was hooked up to a blood-filtering machine. His blood flowed out of one of his arms and through the machine that collected the stem cells. Then his blood—minus the blood-forming stem cells—flowed back into his other arm. This process took about five hours.

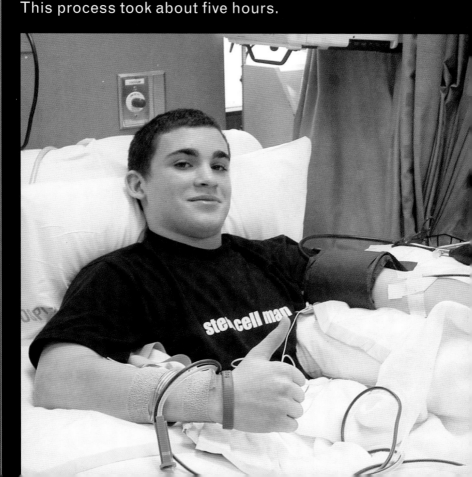

During the time that Nicholas was getting ready to donate his blood-forming stem cells, Paul was getting ready for the transplant. He was given special drugs too. But his drugs were to wipe out any blood-forming stem cells still in his bone marrow. That, of course, meant no new blood cells of any kind were being made. Paul needed frequent transfusions of red blood cells and platelets to stay alive. He was also given medications to protect him from germs. A half-hour after Nicholas donated his blood-forming stem cells, Paul received them. They were injected, like any normal transfusion, directly into the device in his chest. Then his blood carried the donated stem cells throughout his body. They traveled to Paul's bone marrow.

His mother, Diane, said, "We held our breath day after day after that, waiting for Paul's blood tests to show white blood cells again. That would be proof the transplanted stem cells were working." Ten days after the transplant, the first white cells appeared!

With chemotherapy alone, Paul had only a 50 percent chance of remaining in remission. With the transplant, his chances jumped to 70 percent.

37

For the next three weeks, Paul had to stay in the hospital, well away from other people. White blood cells are the body's primary defense against germs. With white blood cells just being formed, the risk of getting sick was high. At the same time, Paul was also given a new treatment that was just being tested. He was given something called monoclonal antibodies.

When germs invade the body, white blood cells produce proteins called antibodies. Different antibodies are made for each kind of invader. These antibodies coat the invaders and stop them. They also attract other white blood cells that destroy the invaders. Monoclonal antibodies are antibodies scientists make in a lab. They make different kinds for different kinds of cancer. The monoclonal antibodies given to Paul were created especially to seek out and destroy any remaining myeloid leukemic cells.

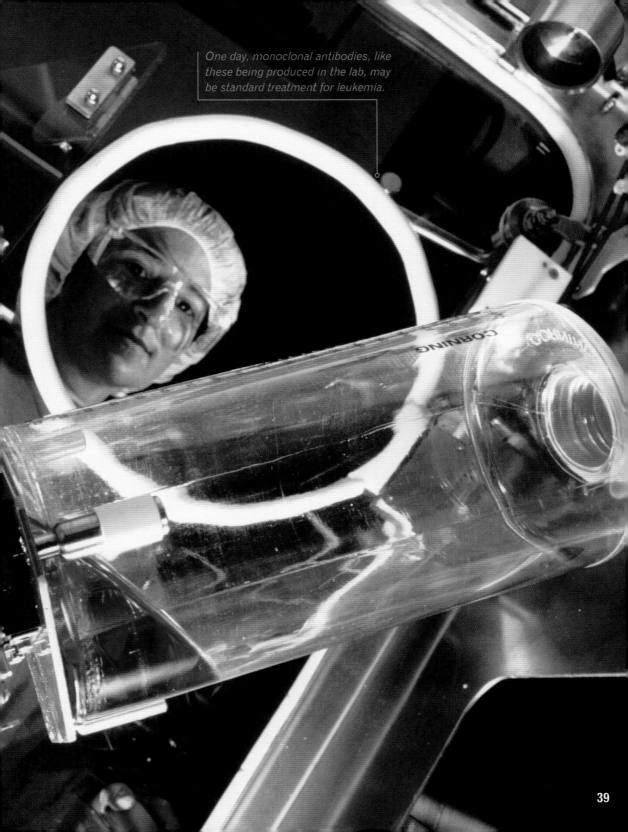

One day, monoclonal antibodies, like these being produced in the lab, may be standard treatment for leukemia.

Eventually, Paul went home to begin his new life. His body's ability to fight diseases, though, was like that of a baby. He got sick often. And he had to repeat all of his childhood vaccinations. Finally, his body became better able to defend against diseases. He was healthier. For the first year or so, he also had blood tests three times a week. These checked for leukemic white blood cells.

Paul said, "Over time, I could go longer between blood tests. It's now been about four years since my transplant, and I only have to go for a blood test every three months. That will eventually taper off to once a year. The best thing is I feel strong again—as strong as I did before I got sick."

IN THE PAST, BLOOD SAMPLES WERE CHECKED BY SOMEONE LOOKING AT THEM UNDER A MICROSCOPE. With this method, only about twenty cells could be checked at a time. Like looking at a pinch of sand on a beach, this view doesn't show what else might be in the rest of the blood. New technologies are helping doctors look for any remaining leukemic cells, following treatment. One technology,

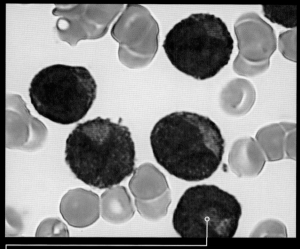

This microscopic view of a blood sample shows leukemic white blood cells (purple). By the time the disease is spotted this way, the patient is probably very sick.

called a flow cytometer, adds special dyes to the blood sample. Each kind of dye only sticks to the surface of a specific kind of blood cell. Then the blood sample is passed through a laser light and analyzed by a computer. It quickly looks at thousands of blood cells and identifies any leukemic cells.

This machine is a flow cytometer.

UPDATES

BIANCA WHITE COMPLETED HER MAINTENANCE CHEMOTHERAPY IN SEPTEMBER 2009. Her mother, Lea, said, "She's in school now and feeling well. Best of all, her blood tests show no signs of leukemia."

PAUL LUISI DIDN'T NEED ANY ADDITIONAL CHEMOTHERAPY AFTER HIS STEM CELL TRANSPLANT. He's in high school and enjoys thinking about what he might want to do in the future. He said, "I look back and think 'I can't believe I went through all this.'"

Bianca enjoys playing again.

Paul still loves sports. He's on his high school's football team.

Diane Luisi said, "Through Paul's battle with AML, we got to know other families whose children were suffering from leukemia. Not everyone has made it, and we are saddened by those who have died. As a parent of a survivor, I know to honor the people we've lost to this disease we need to live strong." The entire Luisi family does that by working hard every year to raise money to support the Pediatric Bone Marrow Transplant program of the Morgan Stanley Children's Hospital, part of New York Presbyterian Hospital.

Medical research is helping doctors give leukemia patients hope for a long and healthy life.

BIANCA'S NECKLACE

Many hospitals around the world have a program called the Beads of Courage. Through this program, children receive beads for completing each step of their treatment. The necklace that's created builds a visual story of what each child has gone through. There are different color beads for different kinds of treatment: a red bead for a blood transfusion, a white bead for every day of chemotherapy, and more. Bianca White's necklace is made up of more than fifty beads. Her favorite is the single purple bead. She

This is Bianca's necklace.

received that bead to mark the day her treatment ended.

BLOOD IS AMAZING!

- Every cell in the human body receives the oxygen and food nutrients it needs from the blood. Blood also carries away the cells' waste products.

- The amount of blood that flows to different parts of the body varies to meet the body's changing needs. For example, blood flow to the active muscles increases while a person is running. After a person eats, blood flow to the stomach and intestinal area goes up.

- Blood travels continually through a system of blood vessels (arteries, capillaries, and veins) that if stretched out could wrap two times around Earth.

GLOSSARY

antibiotic: a drug used to help the body defend itself against invading bacteria

antibodies: special proteins that mark bacteria, viruses, or other invaders so the body's white blood cells can destroy them

biopsy: a study of a sample of a person's blood or body tissue to check for a disease

blood-forming stem cells: cells in the bone marrow that create blood cells—red blood cells, white blood cells, and platelets

bone marrow: the soft, elastic tissue inside the cavities of some bones, such as the hip bones and the long bones of the legs and arms. Blood-forming stem cells in the marrow create blood cells.

chemotherapy: the drug treatment used to kill leukemic and other cancer cells in the body

erythrocyte: a red blood cell

lymphocyte: a white blood cell

monoclonal antibody: a special protein made in a lab to fight leukemia

platelets: a blood cell that forms a clot or a scab to stop bleeding

red blood cell: a kind of blood cell that carries oxygen to all the other body cells

remission: a period when a patient has no signs of a disease in his or her body. In leukemia, remission means that fewer than 5 percent of the cells in a blood sample are leukemic.

thrombocyte: a platelet

transfusion: an injection of whole blood or blood cells

white blood cell: a kind of blood cell that fights infections and disease

MORE INFORMATION

Want to learn more information about leukemia and the latest medical advancements for treating diseases affecting the blood? Check these resources.

BOOKS

Johnson, Rebecca. *Daring Cell Defenders*. Minneapolis: Millbrook Press, 2006. Learn how white blood cells protect the body from disease.

Lilleby, Kathryn Ulberg. *Stevie's New Blood*. Pittsburgh, PA: Oncology Nursing Press, 2000. Follow the story of a young boy with leukemia undergoing a bone marrow transplant, using his sister's bone marrow.

Moehn, Heather. *Everything You Need to Know about When Someone You Know Has Leukemia*. New York: Rosen Publishing Group, 2000. Dig into the effect and aftereffects of treatments for different kinds of leukemia. Also gain insights into the emotions of having the disease or living with a family member who has leukemia.

Schulz, Charles M. *Why, Charlie Brown, Why: A Story about What Happens When a Friend Is Very Ill*. New York: Ballantine Books, 2002. The familiar Charlie Brown gang faces a friend being diagnosed with leukemia. They respond with compassion to the effects of the illness and treatment. This story is also available as a video from Paramount Pictures.

WEBSITES

The Adventures of Captain Chemo
http://www.royalmarsden.org/
captchemo/index.asp
This interactive site has separate sections for teens and younger children. It shares information about all kinds of cancer, including leukemia, diagnostic tests, chemotherapy, possible treatment, and side effects.

Leukemia Stories and Faces
http://www.acor.org/ped-onc/hp/
leukpages.html
Young children and teenagers who have been diagnosed with leukemia share their feelings and experiences while going through treatment.

Planet Cancer
http://www.planetcancer.org/html/
index.php
This site for teenagers shares information about all kinds of cancer and deals with issues of special interest to teens.

SUPPORT ORGANIZATIONS

Leukemia & Lymphoma Society
1311 Mamaroneck Avenue
White Plains, NY 10605
1-800-955-4572
http://www.leukemia.org/hm_lls
Learn more about these diseases and find a chapter near you.

Leukemia Research Foundation
820 Davis Street
Suite 420
Evanston, IL 60201
847-424-0600
http://www.leukemia-research.org
Discover information about the latest
leukemia research projects.

National Marrow Donor Program
3001 Broadway Street NE
Suite 100
Minneapolis, MN 55413-1753
1-800-627-7692
http://www.marrow.org
Find out about the work of this
organization and how your family
could join them in helping leukemia
patients.

SELECTED BIBLIOGRAPHY

BOOKS

Klosterman, Lorrie. *Leukemia*. New York:
Benchmark Books, 2006.

Lilleyman, John S. *Childhood Leukaemia:
The Facts*. Oxford: Oxford University
Press, 2000.

NEWSPAPERS AND JOURNALS

New York Times Company. "Acute
Lymphocytic Leukemia (ALL)," *New
York Times Health Guide*, June 10, 2008.

Le Page, Cecile. "Decoding of a Acute
Myeloid Leukemia Genome." *Human
Genetics*, November 12, 2008.

Marx, Jean. "Molecular Biology:
Cancer's Perpetual Source." *Science
Magazine*, 317 (August 24, 2007) 1,029–
1,031.

WEBSITES

Children's Leukemia Research
Association. N.d. http://www
.childrensleukemia.org/ (November
30, 2009).

Leukemia Research Foundation. 2009.
http://www.leukemia-research.org/
NETCOMMUNITY/Page
.aspx?pid=183&srcid=224 (November
30, 2009).

Leukemia Research Fund. 2009. http://
www.lrf.org.uk/en/1/home.html
(November 30, 2009).

Healthcommunities.com. "Leukemia
Treatment: Oncology Channel." 2009.
http://www.oncologychannel
.com/leukemias/treatment.shtml
(November 30, 2009).

TELEPHONE INTERVIEWS

Dreyer, Zoann, M.D., December 19, 2008.

Horton, Terzah, M.D., December 17, 2008.

Lill, Michael, M.D., December 19, 2008.

Luisi, Diane, December 9, 2008.

Luisi, Paul, January 28, 2009.

Marcus, Judith R., M.D., January 15, 2009.

Miner, Joyce, January 15, 2009.

Nodland, Sonja, M.D., December 11, 2008.

Sullivan, Michael, M.D., December 18, 2008

White, Lea, December 17, 2008.

INDEX

PHOTO CREDITS

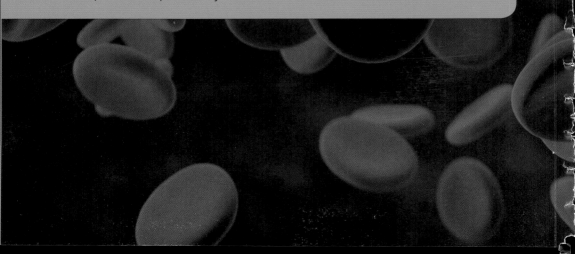